KARATE KATA
AND APPLICATIONS

KARATE KATA
AND APPLICATIONS

VINCE MORRIS
AND
AIDAN TRIMBLE

Crescent Books
New York • Avenel

Aidan: To my sisters and brothers, Margaret, Kathleen, Mary, Joe and Michael

Vince: To my sons, Gareth and Adrian

Stanley Paul & Co. Ltd
An imprint of Random Century Ltd
20 Vauxhall Bridge Road, London SW1V 2SA

Random Century Australia (Pty) Ltd
20 Alfred Street, Milsons Point, Sydney 2061

Random Century New Zealand Limited
PO Box 40-086, Glenfield, Auckland 10

Century Hutchinson South Africa (Pty) Ltd
PO Box 337, Bergvlei 2012, South Africa

© Vince Morris and Aidan Trimble, 1990

ISBN 0-517-12350-9

This 1995 edition published by Crescent Books, distributed by Random House Value Publishing, Inc., 40 Engelhard Avenue , Avenel, New Jersey 07001

Random House
New York • Toronto • London • Sydney • Auckland

A CIP catalog record for this book is available from the Library of Congress

Contents

Acknowledgements

The authors wish to thank the following people for their kindness and helpfulness:

In particular our good friend Keiji Tomiyama, Chief Instructor to Great Britain and Europe for Tani-ha Shito-ryu, for the calligraphy.

Harry Cook for assistance in obtaining the historical photographs.

Chris Hallam and Dave Hook for their help during the photo sequences.

The Sherwood Business and Conference Centre for coffee and room to spread out.

Dominique Shead for calm patience and understanding, plus lunches!

Roddy Bloomfield (well known expert in the art of Real Tennis and erstwhile stunt man) for his enthusiasm for this project.

KATA

Kata

Kata are a predetermined series of blocking, evading and countering techniques against single or multiple attackers, who may be armed or unarmed.

In a sense Kata are not peculiar to Eastern fighting arts. That is to say that the concept of providing an instructional manual is not, for these are to be found in many European languages covering arts ranging from medieval swordsmanship to modern-day boxing.

One element stands out, however, as being significantly different in the Oriental Kata. In the majority of cases the Kata are taught to students by example, only rarely were the early techniques recorded in diagrammatic or textual form, on scrolls which were kept secret and passed on only to exceptional students who had proved themselves worthy after many years practice.

Generally these secret scrolls contained brief details of the main instruction which was passed on orally and by example. They were often presented in a deliberately obscure fashion so as to be of little use if they fell into the hands of someone not well versed in the traditions and teachings of that particular school.

Gichin Funakoshi, the 'Father' of modern karate gives a revealing insight into the emphasis placed upon this secrecy.

In his book *Karate-do Nyumon* published in Japan in 1943 (and owing much to his third son Gigo [Yoshitaka] who is to a great extent responsible for the powerful Shotokan karate of today), Funakoshi relates that in the Ryukyu islands the tradition of secrecy was such that no written records were kept. Techniques were passed on by direct instruction from master to student, very often on a one-to-one basis, and the historical background to the Kata was transmitted by oral tradition, a notoriously imprecise method.

He goes on to tell of a communication he received from an elderly Okinawan karate-ka who wished to pass on to him a particular Kata before he died. As Funakoshi himself could not go, he asked that this Kata be taught to Gigo. After instructing Gigo in the

Kata (behind locked doors in a shuttered room) the old man confessed that he had refused to pass on this Kata to anyone before; only once in a crucially altered way to a man who had continually pestered him until he agreed.

Although in most cases the major concern of the scrolls is to catalogue the techniques of the Ryu, a good proportion of the text is given over to the element which distinguishes them from any Western instructional manual; the interweaving of spiritual philosophy with physical violence!

Based on an eclectic Zen Bhuddhist foundation, with intertwining elements of Confucianism and the native Shinto religion, the art of despatching an enemy was raised to a spiritual level.

A group photo showing karate masters Koyu Konishi (second from right), Gichin Funakoshi (far left) and Kenwa Mabuni (seated), 1934. Mabuni was the founder of Shito-ryu

Indeed, so important was this Zen aspect that the same sentiments appear in scrolls of different Ryu, even in those concerned with distinctly different martial arts, such as Archery and Swordsmanship.

To come to a proper understanding of Kata, and to approach a proper practice of Kata it is vital to appreciate how inextricably interwoven is the philosophical element with the purely pragmatic physical side.

Just as this is so in the Kata of the older classical Ryu, so it is in the relatively younger 'schools' of karate, which have been subsumed into the traditional ethos.

Karate can indeed be practised purely as a strong and effective means of fighting. The Okinawan masters developed techniques capable of inflicting severe damage to any attacker and it is quite possible to train solely in the *waza* – the technique of blocking and counterattacking. Even the early practitioners of the art, however, held the spiritual element to be of equal importance to the physical techniques.

The Okinawan fighting arts were not themselves very much under the influence of the mainland Zen ethos, but *Te,* as the indigenous fighting art was known, became naturally subsumed into the martial culture and its Zen ethic upon its importation into Japan.

Even so, before this time there is evidence that certain Okinawan masters (Higaonna and Itosu, to name two) were much concerned that the art of *Te* be taught as a spiritually-orientated discipline.

After studying the history of karate, and indeed of all of the Japanese fighting arts, one has to conclude that it is a mistake to assume that they are inextricably involved with Buddhism, and with Zen in particular. What becomes clear, however, is that any discipline which removes the fear of death and injury, and enables trained reflexes to deal spontaneously and effectively with any threat is much sought after by the warrior.

The experience of the mainland warrior led to the development of a Zen-permeated martial culture, which, as well as imparting through strict discipline and meditation those very sought after qualities, also encouraged the development of individual values which were morally and socially beneficial: a concern for aesthetics and art, poetry and ceremony, belief in the virtues of honesty, dignity and compassion.

Toward the end of the sixteenth century, for example, the Jigen-ryu martial school, which was essentially concerned with teaching swordsmanship, established a curriculum which as well as concentrating on techniques with sword and dagger also devoted time to practice with spear and bow, and the art of poetry, and the tea ceremony. This was largely due to the influence of the Zen master Zenkicki.

Whether or not many actually attained those qualities which were held to epitomise the 'enlightened' man does not in any way detract from their desirability. The point to reflect upon is that in the original -*jutsu* form or in the later -*do* form a true martial artist is one who has attained mastery of both physical and spiritual aspects.

I have written in greater detail elsewhere *(The Karate-do Manual* and *The Advanced Karate Manual)* of the reasons why this emphasis on the spiritual side came about, but it is of such vital importance to correct understanding and application of Kata that the serious student must be encouraged to learn more of this aspect, and also fully understand that the spirituality – the *Zen* aspect – had a basic pragmatic reason for its emphasis, it made the martial artist a better fighter!

The essence of Zen is a complete acceptance of the inevitability of change; nothing remains the same, the wheel is always turning, leading to the only certainty – at some time or another this human lifespan will come to an end. To place too much importance on this fragile butterfly life was deemed futile; far better to aim at honour and respect, which held society together, even if in pursuance of this it became necessary to give up life. Thus the fighting man defeated his greatest foe – Fear! And specifically the fear of death, which if unconquered could cause that miniscule hesitation in combat that could be fatal.

Hence the importance placed upon gaining 'a mind like water' *(mizu-no-kokoro)* in whose mirror-like surface all actions were reflected and perceived without the ripple of fear to distort the image, allowing the correct response to be made free of all inhibition.

The strict discipline of a continual regime of meditation based upon an acceptance of the transitory nature of all things led the samurai to develop a fearless disregard for the perpetuation of life at all costs, and to foster a strong-willed determination to continue upon a chosen course of action without hesitation, doubt or deflection. Indeed the basis of a formidable fighter!

Anyone, therefore, who wishes to fully understand and gain full benefit from practising the Kata must be prepared to at least con-

*Okinawan karate
master Motabu
showing empi strike*

sider carefully that to practise them purely as physical fitness forms
or simply as a series of physical techniques is to go against the experience, advice and teaching of some of the most fearless and re-
nowned fighters who ever lived!

There are some fifty Kata practised by the various karate schools
today, mostly stemming from the practise and experience of the
old masters, and in the Shotokan style we practice some 26 which
can be broadly categorised into two groups: those which suit the
larger, stronger martial artist, and those which are more appropriate to a lighter, more mobile stature.

The former group, which stress physical strength, were sometimes formally referred to as *Shorei-ryu*, and the latter, which
emphasise speed and agility as *Shorin-ryu*, and although the *Shorei-
ryu* type are particularly effective for physically conditioning the
body it would be wrong to imagine that this was their main func-
tion, or that they were practised without the correct mental and
spiritual concentration *(Zanshin)*.

Likewise, although the two types seem to suit essentially different body types it is a mistake to choose to concentrate solely on the group which, on the surface, would appear most appropriate to your particular build; all the Kata develop a rhythm and co-ordination of movement, and the well-balanced fighter must develop the attributes of both types.

At advanced level it is necessary to select one or two Kata, for in-depth practice, to 'enter deeply' into the soul of the Kata, and at this stage then it would be appropriate to select from the type most suitable to your physical characteristics. Even so the full range of Kata should not be neglected.

The problem

Although the physical practice of the various Kata is in itself an excellent physical exercise, promoting suppleness, flexibility and improved muscle tone, we have seen that this is only part of the story, and that proper practice demands that the martial artist develop *Zanshin* an alert, concentrated awareness of the totality of the situation, with an untroubled 'unstopping' mind allowing complete freedom for appropriate and effective action.

How?

'While performing a Kata, the karate-ka should imagine himself to be surrounded by opponents and be prepared to execute defensive and offensive techniques in any direction.' So urges the late head of the Japan Karate Association, Masatoshi Nakayama, who was himself one of Gichin Funakoshi's students. (*Best Karate*, Kodansha International Ltd, 1981.)

This to a student under the direct instruction of a master in a one-to-one learning environment, I suggest, is easier to comply with than is the case with the vast majority of karate-ka practising today. We have seen that much of what is now included within the Kata has been passed on by oral tradition, subject to misperception, misunderstanding and plain forgetfulness, as well as by the deliberate desire to keep the original meanings secret, known only to a trusted few. Even some techniques which, on the face of it, are self-evident, may not be quite what they seem in the Kata, they – like many of the blocks – may be presented in the reverse of the proper direction.

Also we know that many of the Kata practised today have been deliberately altered to make them more suitable for mass transmission, as well as to make them conform to the more athletic nature of present-day techniques and upon occasion to make the practice of them safer. For example, whilst performing the Kata *Chinte* Kanazawa Sensei broke his right hand by striking the back with *Ipponken* causing Master Nakayama to remind him that the Kata should be modified for training purposes. All of which makes the practice of the Kata in line with Nakayama's advice practically impossible, as, in our experience, the vast majority of students have and can only have a rudimentary understanding of the *Bunkai* – the applications of the techniques contained within the Kata.

Takayuki Kubota, Head of Gosoku-ryu Karate in America (The International Karate Association), and well known as an instructor to Law enforcement agencies writes: 'At the moment most people that practise Kata have no idea of its real meaning, or the benefit that it brings. They practise Kata and Kumite as though they were two different things whereas of course Kumite starts with Kata and Kata starts with Kumite.'*

This being so, it is impossible that the Kata be practised fully and completely, and that proper *Zanshin* be exercised.

Yet another problem must be faced. To be practised as was originally intended, that is as a powerful and *effective* means of self-defence, with value in today's society, then it should be obvious that even if all the original *bunkai* were known practice solely related to them would be anachronistic; having little relevance. Sadly, in the world of today attackers are more likely to wield a razor-knife, broken beer-glass or even a gun than a *bo* or *jo*. This latter problem becomes more apparent when one realises that even within the confines of the history of the development of karate techniques the Kata are anachronistic in that they ignore many of the techniques which are widely (and effectively) incorporated into the basic practice of modern karate. Such techniques as: *mawashi-geri* (roundhouse kick), *ushiro-mawashi-geri* (back roundhouse kick), *kakato-geri* (heel or axe kick) and *ushiro-geri* (back kick) are only a few which do not appear in the Kata.

Indeed, this problem exercised the current head of Shotokan Karate International, Hirokazu Kanazawa, to the extent that he began to incorporate *jodan mawashi-geri* into the Kata *Empi*. This move did not find favour, however, and the Kata is currently practised as before, with no roundhouse kick.

It would seem appropriate at some stage for senior *Sensei* to pool ideas and formulate a new Kata, based on the historic principles, but incorporating modern karate techniques.

---

*Interview with David Chambers in *Fighting Arts* No. 54.

The myth

There is one widespread myth that needs dispelling before we consider the final section of this chapter, the precepts which must be borne in mind when practising the Kata, and that is the racial myth that mastery of karate, and in particular the Kata, is only attainable by the Japanese, for only they can have a real understanding of the martial ethos permeating the art, and can therefore achieve the highest levels of skill.

Frankly this is arrant nonsense!

Let us turn the premise around and hypothesise a native English sport, with philosophical connotations and obscure rules and rituals, deeply rooted in English tradition. Could we then safely assume that no-one but a native-born Englishman would ever excel in the sport, and that no Englishman would ever be beaten by a foreign competitor. Even a cursory glance at the record of the England Cricket team over recent years will serve to underline the ridiculousness of this idea!

Of course there are cogent (financial) reasons for the perpetuation of the myth of Japanese superiority, and indeed there may well be some Japanese who actually believe in it. This does not mean that anyone else need accept it. Indeed, when karate was first introduced to the West, the Japanese were naturally superior, both in skill and understanding, but also in the physical flexibility – especially in the hips and legs – which came to them as a direct consequence of the nature of their society, and which enabled them to have a greater facility in the techniques.

Japanese supremacy has now been challenged, just like the supremacy of English cricketers. At first the Japanese fighters were thought unbeatable, but the records show that the British team has defeated the Japanese on each of the last four occasions when they have fought. The most obvious example is Aidan Trimble's success in Tokyo, the heartland of Japanese karate, when he took on and soundly defeated the best of the world's Shotokan Karate International fighters, including the cream of the Japanese, to become the first World Openweight Kumite Champion.

The point I am going at lengths to make is an important one. If you place any credence in this myth then you set limits to your own progress. There are no limits within the art of karate, only those inherent in each individual practitioner. Believe this and put aside all negative inhibiting ideas.

How to Practise the Kata

As mentioned before, the mental attitude to Kata should be the same as for Kumite. The opponent must actually exist for you, or the Kata will be relegated to the level of mere physical calisthenics. In correct practice it is vital to maintain a sense of urgency and reality, and at every step envisage yourself as actually under threat and attack by a number of assailants determined to do you serious harm.

In this atmosphere *Zanshin* can be developed, and no technique need be 'pulled' short of the target through fear of inflicting damage, as in practice with a partner, and, furthermore, no time can be grabbed for regaining one's breath with these opponents, as they know no rules of fair-play, nor any referee's intervention!

Pragmatically, however, Kata training is a progressive experience which can roughly be defined in three stages.

To begin with, the student has enough to do simply trying to remember the sequence of techniques and changes of direction whilst keeping time to the teacher's count without trying to visualise 'real' opponents.

This is quite in order, for at this stage the technical proficiency and mental awareness are secondary to establishing the pattern of the Kata. Even so, during this process whilst the motor skills and underlying rhythms of the blocking and countering movements are being assimilated, the body is being strengthened, and balance and co-ordination enhanced.

The second stage of development commences when the pattern of the Kata has become firmly established, almost second nature. Now the emphasis is upon specific aims. The student strives to refine his practice, polishing technique and beginning to keep in mind the target areas, the appropriate application of speed and strength, and correct breathing. At this stage, under the direction of an experienced *sensei,* the student is put under increasing physical and mental pressure and begins to become aware of just how important is the power of the mind in physical activity. He or she learns to drag something extra from the depths of the psyche, a strength and stubborness that perhaps has never before been revealed. The body becomes so exhausted from obeying the *sensei*'s command: 'Hai! Now once more!' that it becomes impossible to even keep the eyelids open! Every breath becomes a painful gasp and seemingly must be the last, but even as the body staggers and weakens the spirit shouts: 'I will not give in!' – And from this the lesson is learned that in the depths of your spirit you can never be defeated.

The third stage is properly the practice of 'Moving Zen'. The techniques are by now instinctive and the goal perfection. Practice becomes an intensely private thing, age no longer matters, youthfulness, strength and stamina, even a fully operative body are not prerequisites for this journey. Here the Kata is never for simple display but is a vehicle, a path of absolute determined awareness and concentrated attention.

By this final stage the karate-ka has developed the ability to fuse mind, body and spirit to profound depths. The outward display is secondary to the manifestation of inner power and calm determination. Now the 'stopped' mind is released; fear is defeated by acceptance, and all peripheral anxieties are seen in perspective and set aside as full attention is directed to 'here and now'.

In Karate-do the Kata begin by being concerned with the physical down-to-earths of balance, co-ordination, power, flexibility and so on, but progress to being far, far more.

Each time a Kata is practiced (as a whole or in part – by a karate-ka thoroughly familiar with it) it should be a new creation, fresh, dramatic and meaningful in just the same way that a musician recreates a piece that has long featured in his repertoire. It should never be a stale repetition, a bored and boring rendition.

On the contrary, just as the musician 'loses' himself in his music so the karate-ka re-interprets and re-creates the Kata, bringing it to life and imbuing it with his own personality, making each performance the first.

There are occasions, however, when it is beneficial to perform the Kata in different ways. Hirokazu Kanazawa – one of the foremost karate teachers in the world – advocates that every third time it should be performed without power, directing the attention to maintaining *Hara* (concentrating *Ki* below the navel) and at the same time concentrating on the correct tensing and relaxing of the muscles.

Many teachers also advocate the practice of Kata in the opposite direction to the normal, thus affording practice on both sides and more deeply ingraining the sequence into the memory.

Tokyo University Karate Club training, 1930

Aidan and I both strongly advocate that you vary the direction in the *Dojo* in which you regularly practise. This will help ensure that you concentrate wholly on the Kata and the imaginary opponents rather than using a familiar object in your area of vision to help orientate you. Similarly, after taking care to make sure of safety, you should from time to time practise the Kata with your eyes closed.

For the karate-ka interested in Kata competition these last suggestions will be helpful in overcoming the problem of performing in an unfamiliar environment.

In our book *The Advanced Karate Manual* I gave a comprehensive outline of utilising visualisation techniques as an aid to practice. I will simply point out here that this method can prove invaluable in refining the execution and performance of Kata, and is strongly recommended.

A point worth making to the Kata competitor is that the idea of competition is essentially alien to the fundamental concept of Kata, which we have seen to be not for public display but as an aid to the effective execution of Kumite and self-defense. Following this, as Kanazawa comments, the essence lies not in the beauty of movement but in its efficiency.

In many instances today we find that Kata competitors vie with each other to perform the 'flashiest' most acrobatic Kata, complete with side-kicks that go straight up! Thus underlining how far from a proper understanding of their art are both the competitor and the judges who are impressed by external agility rather than internal condition manifested in simple, effective and efficiently executed techniques performed with *Zanshin*.

As a matter of course the *Bunkai* – the application of the techniques – should form part of regular practice with a partner. To make Kata performance meaningful it is necessary to visualise the attackers and their techniques as they would be in reality, and this means constant practice with partners to enable correct judgment of distance and timing.

To begin with the defenses should be the traditional ones which were originally devised to meet each particular attack. Only when thoroughly conversant with these should the *Bunkai* be altered.

If the Kata are not to be relegated to the status of museum pieces, however, it is important that they be applicable to the different circumstances of the modern age, wherein it is most unlikely that an attacker would wield a six-foot *Bo*, but baseball bat, knife, club or gun. Every type of weapon demands a different response in terms of recognising the potential of the weapon and assessing the correct defense. It is a good idea, therefore, to incorporate various weapons into *Bunkai* practice and modify the responsive technique, distance and timing to suit. Of course, by the nature of the Kata, by the secrecy surrounding them, through misunderstanding and by purposeful deception, and by the changes wrought by a variety of masters, it is not always clear just what the original meaning of any particular move was. If this is the case, then we advise consulting the original from which the Shotokan Kata evolved. This will very often provide the clue and help clarify the original purpose. Failing this, it is better to invent your own application than simply to practise the technique as calisthenics. Bear in mind, however, that the application must be efficient and effective, and follow properly from the one preceding and lead without forcing into the one following.

The precepts

The following points should be borne in mind when practising Kata:

Courtesy: karate begins and ends with courtesy, and is signified with the bow *(rei)* at the start and finish. It is important that the state of *zanshin* is apparent in the demeanour from the moment that the karate-ka walks forward to begin the Kata. The stance: heels touching, toes apart, hands lightly touching the thighs *(musubi-dachi)* should be relaxed but alert, the gaze directed straight ahead. A sense of calm determination should be cultivated as the mind and spirit is prepared for the encounters to come *(yoi no kisin)*.

All Kata should begin and end on the same spot on the line of performance *(embusen)*. Proper mastery is not attained until the breathing is harmonised with the execution of technique and posture *(kokyu)*.

Performing any element of the Kata without understanding turns it into an exercise in calisthenics and devalues the practice. You should always bear in mind the application and defend or attack the correct target areas *(tyakugan)* accordingly.

An error that we see quite often is the application of too much force and *kime*. It is important to understand that the Kata contain many movements which do not demand this. Master Funakoshi himself points out: 'The use of strength in continuous, rapid motions does not mean that one is skilled' *(Karate-do Kyohan)*. You must move quickly or slowly as necessary, and only apply strength where appropriate.

Remember that *Yame* at the end of a Kata carries the implication of a continuing state of readiness, so do not 'switch off'. To the true martial artist there is no dividing line between their art and 'real-life'. The art becomes the shaping and refining tool for moulding life, and in turn becomes inextricably an expression of that life. There can be, then, no 'switching off' until life ends.

Pragmatically of course, a state of unawareness has often brought about the sudden end of life!

Key

It is impossible to learn kata only from a book. A good instructor is vital. Diagrams and text should serve as aids to memory. This being so, the direction of movement has been indicated by what should be self-explanatory symbols, which indicate general movement, not necessarily the focus of attention.

NB: All Kata begin and end with the bow of respect *(Rei).*

KATA
AND APPLICATIONS

Heian Shodan

This is now the first proper Kata in the Shotokan syllabus, in which training is given in basic and essential techniques: the stances *Zen-kutsu-dachi* and *Kokutsu-dachi*, the blocks *Gedan-barai, Age-uke* and *Shuto-uke*. The Kata contains 21 movements, and takes approximately 40 seconds to perform. It should not be rushed. Pay attention to the rhythm of the movements.

Heian Shodan

STEP BY STEP

1. *Shizentai*

2. *Musubi-Dachi*

3. *Rei*

8.

9. *Zenkutsu-Dachi Oi-Zuki*

10.

11. *Zenkutsu-Dachi Gedan-Barai*

16.

17. *Zenkutsu-Dachi Gedan-Barai*

18.

19. *Zenkutsu-Dachi Age-Uke*

4. Yoi

5.

6.

7. Zenkutsu-Dachi
Gedan-Barai

12.

13. Tetsu-Uchi

14.

15. Zenkutsu-Dachi
Oi-Zuki

20. Zenkutsu-Dachi
Age-Uke

KIAI

21. Zenkutsu-Dachi
Age-Uke. Kiai!

22.

23. Zenkutsu-Dachi
Gedan-Barai

24. Zenkutsu-Dachi
Oi-Zuki

25.

26. Zenkutsu-Dachi
Gedan-Barai

27. Zenkutsu-Dachi
Oi-Zuki

KIAI

32. Zenkutsu-Dachi
Oi-Zuki. Kiai!

33.

34. Kokutsu-Dachi
Shuto-Uke

35.

40. Kokutsu-Dachi
Shuto-Uke

41. Yame

28.

29. *Zenkutsu-Dachi*
Gedan-Barai

30. *Zenkutsu-Dachi*
Oi-Zuki

31. *Zenkutsu-Dachi*
Oi-Zuki

36. *Kokutsu-Dachi*
Shuto-Uke

37.

38. *Kokutsu-Dachi*
Shuto-Uke

39.

Figs 11-13 *Disengagement to hammerfist strike*

Figs 11-13 *(alternative bunkai) Forearm block to hammersmith strike*

Figs 18-19 *Openhand block, wrist grab, forearm strike to elbow*

Figs 38-40 *Knifehand block to knifehand strike*

d

Heian Shodan
SEQUENCES

Figs 1-10

Figs 11-22

Figs 23-34

Figs 35-41

平安弐段

Heian Nidan

This second training Kata gives further practice in the difficult backstance *Kokutsu-dachi*, rapid execution of consecutive techniques in one stance, simultaneous blocking and kicking whilst balanced on one leg etc., to a more complex rhythm than the first Kata.

It introduces many new techniques such as: *Mae-geri* and *Yoko-geri*, *Haiwan jodan-uke*, *Uraken-uchi* and *Shihon nukite*.

Containing 26 movements, this Kata should take approximately 50-60 seconds to perform.

Heian Nidan

STEP BY STEP

1. *Shizentai*

2. *Musubi-Dachi*

3. *Rei*

8. *Kokutsu-Dachi Chudan-Zuki*

9. *Kokutsu-Dachi*

10. *Kokutsu-Dachi Right Jodan Haiwan-Uke Left Ude-Soete*

11. *Kokutsu-Dachi Right Nagashi-Uke Left Tetsui-Uc.*

16. *Kokutsu-Dachi Shuto-Uke*

17. *Kokutsu-Dachi Shuto-Uke*

18. *Kokutsu-Dachi Shuto-Uke*

19.

20. *Zenkutsu-Dachi Nihon-Nukite. Kiai!*

21.

4. *Yoi*

5.

6. *Kokutsu-Dachi Left Jodan Haiwan-Uke Right Ude-Soete*

7. *Kokutsu-Dachi Left Nagashi-Uke Right Tetsui-Uchi*

12. *Kokutsu-Dachi Chudan-Zuki*

13.

14. *Yoko-Geri-Keage Uraken*

15.

22. *Kokutsu-Dachi Shuto-Uke*

23. *Kokutsu-Dachi Shuto-Uke*

24. *Kokutsu-Dachi Shuto-Uke*

25. *Kokutsu-Dachi Shuto-Uke*

26. *Zenkutsu-Dachi Left Gedan Shuto-Uke*

26a *Front view of Fig. 26*

27. *Zenkutsu-Dachi*

27a. *Front view of Fig. 27*

30 *Zenkutsu-Dachi*

30a. *Front view of Fig. 30*

31. *Zenkutsu-Dachi*

32. *Zenkutsu-Dachi Left Uchi-Uke*

38. *Zenkutsu-Dachi Gedan-Barai*

39.

40. *Zenkutsu-Dachi Age-Uke*

41.

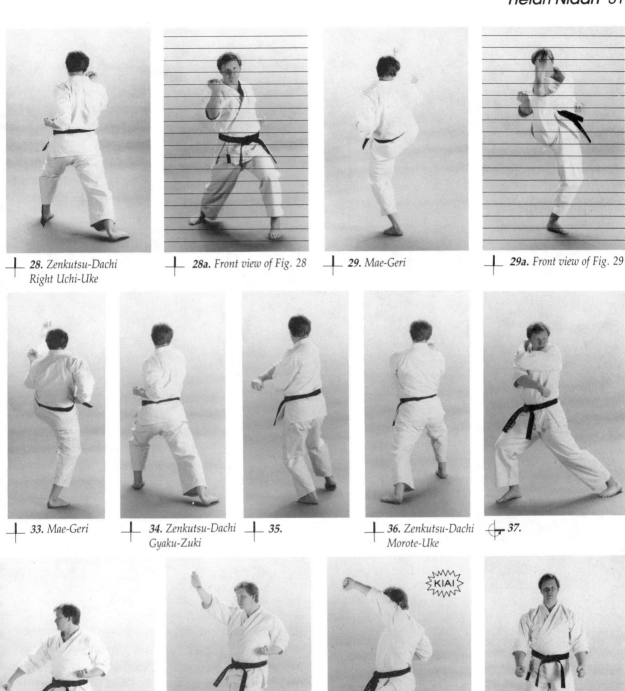

28. *Zenkutsu-Dachi Right Uchi-Uke*	**28a.** *Front view of Fig. 28*	**29.** *Mae-Geri*	**29a.** *Front view of Fig. 29*

33. *Mae-Geri*	**34.** *Zenkutsu-Dachi Gyaku-Zuki*	**35.**	**36.** *Zenkutsu-Dachi Morote-Uke*	**37.**

42. *Zenkutsu-Dachi Gedan-Barai*	**43.**	**44.** *Zenkutsu-Dachi Age-Uke. Kiai!*	**45.** *Yame*

KIAI

Heian Nidan
APPLICATIONS

a

b

Figs 6-8 a. Block

b. Deflection and strike to elbow

a

Figs 6-8 (alternative bunkai) **a.** Block

b

b. Arm lock

c

c. Back fist or hammer fist

a

Figs 13-16

b

b. Block and side snap kick to head

c

Fig 26 Straight fingers strike

a

Figs 26-29 Scooping block and mae-geri

b

c. Straight punch or hammer fist

a

b

Figs 19-20 *Pressing block and straight fingers strike*

d. Back elbow strike

e

e. Alternative block and side kick to midsection
(alternative bunkai to b)

a

b

Figs 43-44 *Parry and rising forearm strike*

Heian Nidan

SEQUENCES

Figs 1-10

Figs 11-22

Figs 23-34

Figs 35-45

Heian Sandan

This Kata introduces one of the most difficult stances to master, *Kiba-dachi,* and continues training in multiple techniques from one stance. It gives practice in defending with the feet and elbows if the arms are restrained, and a response to an attack from the rear.

There are 20 movements in this Kata, which should take approximately 40 seconds to perform.

Heian Sandan

STEP
BY
STEP

1. *Shizentai*

2. *Musubi-Dachi*

3. *Rei*

8. *Heisoku-Dachi*
Kosa-Uke

9.

10. *Kosa-Uke*

11.

16. *Heisoku-Dachi*
Kosa-Uke

17.

18. *Kokutsu-Dachi*
Left Chudan Morote-Uke

19. *Left Osae-Uke*

_|_ **4.** *Yoi*

_|_ **5.**

_|_ **6.** *Kokutsu-Dachi Left Uchi-Uke*

_|_ **7.** *Heisoku-Dachi*

_|_ **12.** *Kokutsu-Dachi Right Uchi-Uke*

_|_ **13.** *Heisoku-Dachi*

_|_ **14.** *Heisoku-Dachi Kosa-Uke*

_|_ **15.**

_|_ **20.** *Zenkutsu-Dachi Right Chudan Shihon Nukite*

_|_ **21.** *Turn*

_|_ **22.** *Turn*

_|_ **23.** *Kiba-Dachi*

24. Kiba-Dachi Left Chudan Tetsui-Uchi

25. Step forward

26. Zenkutsu-Dachi Oi-Zuki. Kiai!

KIAI

27. Turn

30a. Front view of Fig. 30

31.

31a. Front view of Fig. 31

32. Kiba-Dachi Right Jodan Uraken-Uchi

35. Kiba-Dachi Left Empi-Uke

36.

37. Kiba-Dachi Left Jodan Uraken-Uchi

38. Kiba-Dachi

28. *Heisoku-Dachi*
Ryoken Koshi Gamae

29. *Mikazuki-Geri*
Fumikomi

29a. *Front view of Fig. 29*

30. *Kiba-Dachi*
Right Empi-Uke

32a. *Front view of Fig. 32*

33. *Kiba-Dachi*

33a. *Side view of Fig. 33*

34.

39. *Right Mikazuki-Geri*
Fumikomi

40. *Kiba-Dachi*
Right Empi-Uke

41.

42. *Kiba-Dachi*
Right Jodan Uraken-Uchi

43.

44.

44a. *Front view of Fig. 44*

45.

48. *Step up*

49. *Turn*

50. *Kiba-Dachi Right Tate-Zuki Left Ushiro-Empi*

51. *Kiba-Dachi Right Tate-Zuki Left Ushiro Empi. Kiai*

45a. *Front view of Fig. 45*

46. *Kiba-Dachi*
Right Tate Shuto-Uke

46a. *Front view of Fig. 46*

47. *Zenkutsu-Dachi*
Left Oi-Zuki

52.

53. *Yame*

Heian Sandan
APPLICATIONS

 *a*

 *b*

Figs 6-8 Block and disengagement from grab

 *a*

 *b*

 *c*

Figs 6-8 (alternative bunkai) Disengagement from double lapel grab and counter with backfist to face and simultaneous

 *a*

 *b*

 *c*

Figs 20-24 Spinning defence against grab or twisting arm-lock

 *a*

 *b*

 *c*

punch to stomach

Figs 20-24 (*alternative bunkai*) *Elbow strike to groin followed by shoulder wheel throw*

Figs 23-26 *Blocking attack – stamping kick counter. Blocking attack – back fist strike*

Figs 39-42 *Elbow and punch defence to grab from rear*

Figs 39-42 *(alternative bunkai) Lunge punch attack followed by shoulder throw*

Heian Sandan

SEQUENCES

Figs 1-10

Figs 11-22

KIAI

Figs 23-34

Figs 35-46

KIAI

Figs 47-53

Heian Yondan

Here the Kata more obviously begins to assume the characteristics of the traditional Kata from which it was drawn. It gives practice in the varieties of rhythm inherent in karate, the slow increase in tension on the one hand and the explosive release of powerful techniques on the other. Some of the more dangerous techniques of the traditional Kata are re-introduced, *Hiza-geri* to the opponent's face for example.

Comprising 27 movements, this Kata should take approximately 50 seconds to perform.

**1.** Shizentai

**2.** Musubi-Dachi

**3.** Rei

_**8.** Kokutsu-Dachi
Kaishu Haiwan-Uke_

**9.** Turn

_**10.** Zenkutsu-Dachi
Gedan Juji-Uke_

**11.** Step forward

_**16.** Heisoku-Dachi
Koshi-Gamae_

_**17.** Yoko-Geri Keage
Uraken-Uchi_

_**18.** Zenkutsu-Dachi
Left Empi-Uchi_

_**19.** Zenkutsu-Dachi
Left Shuto Gedan-Barai_

4. Yoi

5. Kokutsu-Dachi

6. Kokutsu-Dachi
Kaishu Haiwan-Uke

7. Kokutsu-Dachi

12. Kokutsu-Dachi
Right Chudan Morote-Uke

13. Heisoku-Dachi
Koshi Gamae

14. Yoko-Geri Keage
Uraken-Uchi

15. Zenkutsu-Dachi
Right Empi-Uchi

20. Zenkutsu-Dachi
Right Jodan Shuto-Uchi

21. Right Jodan Mae-Geri

22. Te-Osae-Uke

23. Kosa-Dachi
Right Uraken-Uchi. Kiai!

24. Turn
Kokutsu-Dachi

25. Kokutsu-Dachi

26. Kokutsu-Dachi
Chudan Kakiwake-Uke

27. Right Jodan Mae-Geri

32. Left Mae-Geri

33. Zenkutsu-Dachi
Left Oi-Zuki

34. Zenkutsu-Dachi
Right Gyaku-Zuki

35. Turn

39a Front view of Fig. .

40. Right Hiza-Ate. Kiai!

KIAI

40a Front view of Fig. 40

41. Turn

28. *Zenkutsu-Dachi Chudan Oi-Zuki*

29. *Zenkutsu-Dachi Left Gyaku-Zuki*

30. *Turn*

31. *Kokutsu-Dachi Chudan Kakiwake-Ure*

36. *Kokutsu-Dachi Left Chudan Morote-Uke*

37. *Kokutsu-Dachi Right Chudan Morote-Uke*

38. *Kokutsu-Dachi Left Chudan Morote-Uke*

39. *Zenkutsu-Dachi Morote Kubi Osae*

42. *Kokutsu-Dachi Left Shuto-Uke*

43. *Kokutsu-Dachi Right Shuto-Uke*

44. *Yame*

Heian Yondan
APPLICATIONS

a

b

Figs 5-6 Block to knife hand strike

a

b

c

Figs 10-12 Block kick and disengage from wrist grab and push

a

b

c

Figs 13-15 Simultaneous block and counter followed by elbow strike

a

b

c

Figs 19-23 a.b. Block kick and counter with knife-hand strike

c.d.e. Front kick,

Fig 6 *(alternative bunkai) Simultaneous block and backhand strike*

e

e

press down punching attack and counter with backfist strike

Figs 19-23 *(alternative bunkai) Deflect kick, block punch and apply armlock follow front kick*

Figs 24-29 *Force apart opponent's arm and counter with front kick and two punches*

Figs 38-42 *From double block slide in and deflect punch, grab head and deliver knee smash. Follow by back elbow strike*

e

f

e

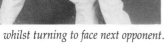

whilst turning to face next opponent.

Heian Yondan

SEQUENCES

Figs 1-10

Figs 11-22

Figs 23-34

Figs 35-44

Heian Godan

The final Kata in the training Kata series, as would be expected, gives practice in a variety of advanced techniques including successive upper and lower blocks *Gedan Juji-uke, Jodan Haishu Juji-uke,* and *Chudan Osae-uke*, plus distinct changes of height and rhythm. A bold-spirited Kata exemplifying the Shotokan spirit.

Containing 23 movements, the Kata should take about 45-50 seconds to perform.

Heian Godan

STEP BY STEP

+ **1.**

+ **2.** *Heisoku-Dachi*

+ **3.** *Rei*

+ **8.** *Heisoku-Dachi*
Left Kagi Gamae

+ **9.** *Kokutsu-Dachi*
Right Uchi-Uke

+ **10.** *Kokutsu-Dachi*
Left Gyaku-Zuki

+ **11.**

+ **16.**

+ **17.** *Zenkutsu-Dachi*
Jodan Haishu-Juji-Uke

+ **18.**

+ **19.** *Zenkutsu-Dachi*
Chudan Osae-Uke

┼ **4.** *Yoi*

┼ **5.** *Kokutsu-Dachi Left Uchi-Uke*

┼ **6.** *Kokutsu-Dachi Right Gyaku-Zuki*

┼ **7.** *Turn*

┼ **12.** *Heisoku-Dachi Right Kagi-Gamae*

┼ **13.** *Kokutsu-Dachi Right Chudan Morote-Uke*

┼ **14.** *Step forward*

┼ **15.** *Zenkutsu-Dachi Gedan Juji-Uke*

┼ **20.** *Step forward*

KIAI

┼ **21.** *Zenkutsu-Dachi Oi-Zuki Chudan. Kiai!*

┼ **22.** *Mikazuki-Geri Fumikomi*

┼ **23.** *Kiba-Dachi Right Gedan-Barai*

┼ **24.** *Turn*

┼ **25.** *Kiba-Dachi*
    Chudan Haishu-Uke

┼ **26.** *Mikazuki Geri*

┼ **27.** *Step forward*

┼ **32.** *Turn*

⊕ **33.** *Jump. Kiai!*

┼ **34.** *Kosa-Dachi*
    Gedan Juji-Uke

┼ **35.** *Turn*

┼ **40.** *Kokutsu-Dachi*
    Manji-Gamae

┼ **41.** *Heisoku-Dachi*
    Manji-Gamae

┼ **42.** *Turn*

┼ **43.** *Heisoku-Dachi*
    Manji-Gamae

28. Kiba-Dachi
Right Empi-Uchi

29. Turn

30. Kosa-Dachi
Chudan Morote-Uke

31. Reinoji-Dachi
Koho-Zuki Age

36. Zenkutsu-Dachi
Right Morote-Uke

37. Turn

38. Zenkutsu-Dachi Left Nagashi-
Uke Right Gedan Shuto-Uchi

39.

44.

45. Zenkutsu-Dachi
Right Nagashi- Uke
Left Gedan Shuto-Uchi

46.

47. Yame

a *b*

Figs 6-8 *Block-counter punch. Grasp attacking arm and strike to elbow*

a *b*

Figs 6-8 *(alternative bunkai) Grasp attacking arm and apply armlock*

a *b* *c*

Figs 15-21 *Block kick, block punch. Twist arm to unbalance opponent, palm-heel strike followed by lunge-punch*

a *b* *c*

with forearm

Figs 29-31 Block punch and strike to jaw

Figs 30-32 Block punch and simultaneously strike to jaw. Block second punch, grasp arm and throw

Figs 37-41 a.b.c. *Deflect punch and strike to groin*

Figs 37-41 *(alternative bunkai) Block punch and counter with palm heel strike to groin. Block second punch and counter with hammer-*

Figs 37-41 *(alternative bunkai) Block kick, then block punch, simultaneously strike to groin, grasp, lift and throw*

d.e. *Grasp and throw attacker*

fist strike to ribs, simultaneously sweeping attacker's front leg

Heian Godan

SEQUENCES

Figs 1-10

Figs 11-22

Figs 23-34

Figs 35-46

Fig 47

Tekki Shodan

Ankoh (Yasutsune) Itosu, an Okinawan karate master, revised and adapted older Kata. Himself a student of the legendary Sokon Matsumura, Itosu was the great formulator and developer of Kata, and according to Funakoshi it was from Master Itosu that he learned the *Heian* and three *Tekki* Kata amongst others.

He specialised in the Tekki Kata and made Funakoshi spend three years learning each, admonishing that they were at once the easiest to learn but also the most difficult to learn.

The original name *Naihanchi* was changed to *Tekki* by Funakoshi, and although *Tekki Shodan* is an old *Shuri-te* Kata, *Nidan* and *Sandan* were created by Itosu as strengthening and training Kata, basing them upon the original but eliminating the dangerous techniques.

Originally performed in Naihanchi-dachi and Hachi-ji-dachi, they are now all performed in Kiba-dachi.

One of the most difficult techniques to perform correctly in *Tekki Shodan* is *Nami-gaeshi* the 'Returning wave' deflection. Many students incorrectly slap the instep against the inside of the thigh. The foot should travel to the front of the thigh to block or deflect a kicking attack.

The *Tekki* Kata should be practised assiduously in order to promote flexibility and lower body strength.

Tekki Shodan

STEP BY STEP

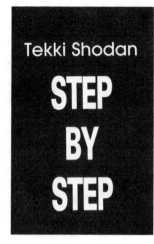

1. *Shizentai*

2. *Musubi-Dachi*

3. *Rei*

9. *Kiba-Dachi*
Koshi-Gamea

10. *Kiba-Dachi*
Gedan-Barai

11. *Kiba-Dachi*
Right Kagi-Zuki

12. *Kosa-Dachi*

17. *Kiba-Dachi*
Left Jodan Ura-Zuki

18.

19. *Left Nami-Ashi*
(Nami-Gaeshi)

20. *Kiba-Dachi*
Sokumen-Uke

4. *Yoi*

5. *Kosa-Dachi*

6. *Fumikomi*

7. *Kiba-Dachi*
Haishu-Uke

8. *Kiba-Dachi*
Sokumen Empi

13. *Fumikomi*

14. *Kiba-Dachi*
Right Uchi-Uke

15.

16. *Kiba-Dachi*
Jodan Nagashi-Uke

21.

22. *Right Nami-Ashi*
(Nami-Gaeshi)

23. *Kiba-Dachi*
Sokumen-Uke

24. *Kiba-Dachi*
Koshi-Gamae

25. *Kiba-Dachi Morote-Zuki. Kiai!*

26. *Kiba-Dachi*

27. *Kiba-Dachi Haishu-Uke*

28. *Kiba-Dachi Sokumen-Empi*

33. *Fumikomi*

34. *Kiba-Dachi Left Uchi-Uke*

35.

36. *Kiba-Dachi Right Jodan Nagashi-Uke*

41.

42. *Left Nami-Ashi (Nami-Gaeshi)*

43. *Kiba-Dachi Right Sokumen-Uke*

44. *Kiba-Dachi Koshi-Gamae*

29. *Kiba-Dachi*
Koshi-Gamae

30. *Kiba-Dachi*
Right Gedan-Barai

31. *Kiba-Dachi*
Left Kagi-Zuki

32. *Kosa-Dachi*

37. *Kiba-Dachi*
Right Jodan Ura-Zuki

38.

39. *Right Nami-Ashi*
(Nami-Gaeshi)

40. *Kiba-Dachi*
Right Sokumen-Uke

45. *Kiba-Dachi*
Morote-Zuki. Kiai!

46.

47.

48. *Yame*

Tekki Shodan
APPLICATIONS

a   **b**

Figs 6-7 Deflect punch attack grasp arm and attack with stamping kick to knee

a   **b**   **c**

Figs 7-8 Block punch, grab opponent, elbow strike

a   **b**   **c**

Figs 32-35 Block punch, simultaneously counter punch to stomach whilst blocking second punch. Strike to jaw with back fist

b *c*

Figs 28-29 Block punch counter with hook punch

Figs 36-37 a. Block kick attack *b.* Block punch attack

Figs 36-37 (alternative bunkai) Snap up
foot to avoid sweep attack, slide in to
form follow-up spinning back kick

Tekki Shodan
SEQUENCES

Figs 1-10

Figs 11-22

Figs 23-34

Figs 35-46

Figs 47 and 48

Bassai-Dai

A strong, powerful Kata, and one of the earliest, also called Passai. The techniques contained are not vastly more difficult than those already mastered in the *Heian* Kata, but implying the concept of strength and will strong enough to storm a fortress, this Kata exemplifies the idea of changing disadvantage – an initial attack – into advantage by strong and courageous response.

Although a Kata containing many vigorous elements, it is from the *Shorin-ryu*, and therefore the feeling of the Kata should be of precise, fast execution of technique, with due attention given to the appropriate balance between speed and power.

Containing 42 movements, the Kata should take just over a minute to perform.

Bassai-Dai
STEP
BY
STEP

+ *1. Shizentai*

+ *2. Musubi-Dachi*

+ *3. Rei*

+ *8. Zenkutsu-Dachi*
Left Chudan-Uchi-Uke

+ *9.*

+ *10. Zenkutsu-Dachi Gyaki-*
Hanmi Chudan Uchi-Uke

+ *11. Turn*

+ *16.*

+ *17. Zenkutsu-Dachi*
Right Chudan Soto-Uke

+ *18.*

+ *19. Zenkutsu-Dachi Gyaki-*
Hanmi Chudan Uchi-Uke

4. Heisoku-Dachi

5.

6. Kosa-Dachi
Right Uchi-Uke

7. Turn

12. Zenkutsu-Dachi Gyaku-
Hanmi Chudan Soto-Uke

13.

14. Zenkutsu-Dachi
Right Chudan Uchi-Uke

15. Gedan Sukui-Uke

20.

21. Shizentai
Koshi-Gamae

22. Shizentai Left
Chudan Tate Shuto-Uke

23. Shizentai
Right Chudan-Zuki

24.

25. Right Chudan Uchi-Uke

26. Shizentai Left Chudan Zuki

27.

28. Left Chudan Uchi-Uke

33. Kokutsu-Dachi Right Shuto-Uke

34. Kokutsu-Dachi (step-back) Left Shuto-Uke

35.

36. Right Tsukami-Uke Left Soete

41. Heisoku-Dachi. Step back

41a. Front view of Fig. 41

42.

29.

30. Step forward

31. Kokutsu-Dachi
Right Shuto-Uke

32. Kokutsu-Dachi
Left Shuto-Uke

37.

38. Gedan Fumikomi

39. Turn Kokutsu-
Dachi Left Chudan Shuto-Uke

40. Kokutsu-Dachi
Right Chudan Shuto-Uke

42a. Front view of Fig. 42

43. Heisoku-Dachi
Morote-Age-Uke

43a. Front view of Fig. 43

44.

44a. *Front view of Fig. 44*

45. *Zenkutsu-Dachi Chudan Tetsui-Hasami-Uchi*

45a. *Front view of Fig. 45*

46. *Zenkutsu-Dachi. Slide forward Right Chudan Oi-Zuki*

50. *Kiba-Dachi Left Chudan Haishu-Uke*

50a. *Side view of Fig. 50*

51. *Right Mikazuki-Geri*

52. *Kiba-Dachi Right Empi-Uchi*

54a. *Side view of Fig. 54*

55. *Kiba-Dachi. Right Gedan-Barai Left Soete*

55a. *Side view of Fig. 55*

56. *Turn. Zenkutsu-Dachi Koshi Gamae*

46a. *Front view of Fig. 46*

47. *Turn*
Mikazuki-Geri

48. *Kiba-Dachi*
Right Gedan-Barai

49. *Turn*

52a. *Side view of Fig. 52*

53. *Kiba-Dachi. Right*
Gedan-Barai Left Soete

53a. *Side view of Fig. 53*

54. *Kiba-Dachi. Left*
Gedan Barai Right Soete

56a. *Side view of Fig. 56*

57. *Zenkutsu-Dachi*
Yama Zuki

57a. *Side view of Fig. 57*

58. *Heisoku-Dachi*
Koshi-Gamae

├── **58a.** *Side view of Fig. 58*   ├── **59.** *Mikazuki-Geri*   ├── **59a.** *Side view of Fig. 59*   ├── **60.** *Zenkutsu-Dachi Yama-Zuki*

├── **62a.** *Side view of Fig. 62*   ├── **63.** *Zenkutsu-Dachi Yama Zuki*   ├── **63a.** *Side view of Fig. 63*   ⊕── **64.** *Turn*

├── **69.** *Zenkutsu-Dachi Left Gedan Sukui-Uke*   ├── **70.** *Half-step*   ├── **71.** *Kokutsu-Dachi Chudan Shuto-Uke*   ├── **72.** *Turn*

60a. *Side view of Fig. 60*

61. *Heisoku-Dachi Koshi-Gamae*

61a. *Side view of Fig. 61*

62. *Mikazuki-Geri*

65.

66. *Zenkutsu-Dachi Right Gedan Sukui-Uki*

67.

68.

73. *Half-step*

74. *Kokutsu-Dachi Chudan Shuto-Uke. Kiai!*

KIAI

75.

76. *Yame*

Bassai-Dai
APPLICATIONS

Figs 5-6 As opponent attacks slide in and jam attack, simultaneously strike to jaw

Figs 7-10 Block punch, deflect and block second punch, grasp opponent and attack with front kick to stomach or groin

Figs 15-19 (alternative bunkai) With scooping block, hook away attacking leg, block punch and finish with kick to stomach

Figs 15-16 Block kick with scooping block and counter with palm heel strike

Figs 22-29 Block punch with knife-hand block, punch to midsection, with the same arm deflect attacker's arm and punch

Figs 34-38 Block punch, block second punch. Grasp attacker's arm and counter with thrust kick to inside of knee

Figs 34-38 (alternative bunkai) Block punch, grasp and twist arm, counter with thrust kick to hip joint

again to midsection, snapping fist up to strike attacker's face

Figs 35-36 *Opponent grasps your wrists. Trap his hand on yours, in a clockwise circular motion cut into his wrist joint with your knife-hand*

a   *b*   *c*

Figs 42-46 *Block punch or disengage from double lapel grab. Attack double hammer-fist strike followed by lunge punch*

a   *b*   *c*

Figs 47-48 *Draw back blocking punch, spin and attack opponent's head with crescent kick and strike opponent's elbow with your forearm*

a   *b*

Figs 59-60 *Block kick with inside of shin and simultaneously counter-punch to jaw and groin*

a

Figs 50-55 Block punch attack and counter with crescent kick, elbow strike to solar plexus and bottom-fist strike to groin. Block

punch and strike again to groin

Figs 70-72 Deflect punch, step in and strike to throat, sweep opponent to rear

Bassai-Dai

SEQUENCES

Figs 1-10

Figs 11-22

Figs 23-34

Figs 35-46

Figs 47-58

Figs 59-70

Figs 71-77

Kanku-Dai

This Kata was one favoured by Master Funakoshi, who often used it to demonstrate the 'new' art of Karate, stating that it contained all of the art's essential elements.

A Chinese envoy Koshokun (Kong Su Kung) who was an expert in Kendo introduced the Kata Kushanku to Okinawa, teaching the original form to a local expert in the Shuri-te style, Tode Sakugawa, and from that stems the current Shotokan versions of *Kanku-Dai* and *Kanku-Sho*. Known also as *Kwanku*, the Japanese name means 'To look at the sky', referring to the opening movement where the open hands come together with the fingers of the right placed on the back of the left, with the thumbs touching. The hands are then slowly raised above the head, break apart, and in a circular movement are lowered to come together again in front of the body. As the hands are raised the gaze is directed through the triangular gap formed between the hands.

There is a double significance to this opening movement. On the practical level it can be interpreted as a double rising block and groin defence, on the philosophical level it signifies the concept of form becoming emptiness and emptiness becoming form, *'Shiki soku ze ku, ku soku ze shiki'* an important concept in understanding proper practice. The act of directing full attention through the small triangular space concentrates and focusses the mind, the trivial and unimportant are ignored, demanding that one's whole being is centred on a true perception of reality and calm recognition of what is required to interact properly with this.

As an aside to this, and to offer a comment on how Karate-do can be used as an aid to the disadvantaged in society, I quote the remarks of Dirk Robertson a former student, now one of the Federation of Shotokan Karate's instructors who has specialised in working with the physically handicapped:

'If you take the triangle in the Kata and substitute it [with] being handicapped, then one can see where [just as] it is difficult but necessary to concentrate on the triangle, so it is difficult but necessary to accept yourself for what you are . . . seeing everything . . . as it really is, not as you would like to see it, and tackling that with spirit and honesty – the way a Kata should be performed.'

Thus, just as with the able-bodied karate-ka, the Kata are used as a vehicle for self-expression and the development of potential.

The suffix *-Dai* indicates 'Greater' as compared with '*-Sho*' denoting 'Lesser', the latter being created by Yasutsune Itosu using the former as a model.

STEP BY STEP

1. *Shizentai*

2. *Musubi-Dachi Rei*

3. *Yoi*

8.

9.

10. *Kokutsu-Dachi Kaishu-Haiwan-Uke*

11. *Turn*

16.

17. *Right Chudan Uchi-Uke*

18. *Shizentai Left Chudan Zuki*

19.

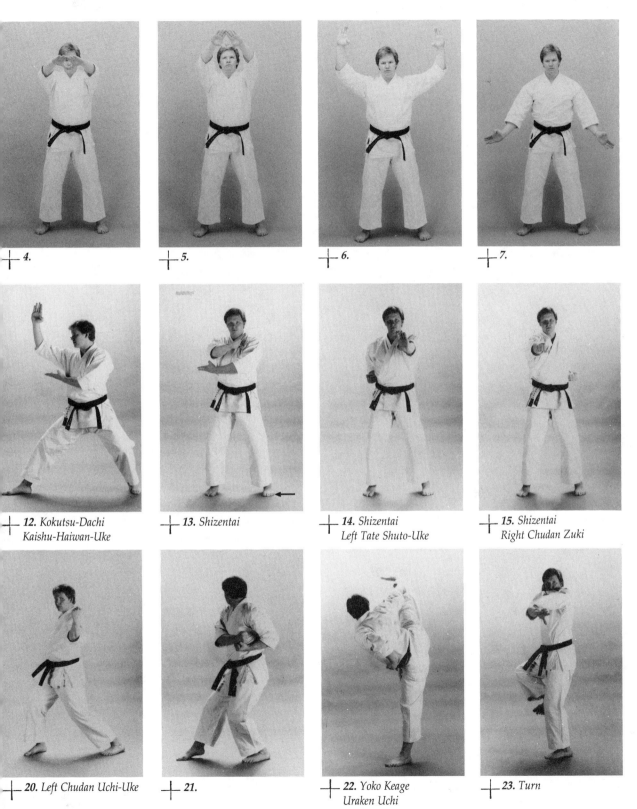

4.

5.

6.

7.

12. Kokutsu-Dachi
Kaishu-Haiwan-Uke

13. Shizentai

14. Shizentai
Left Tate Shuto-Uke

15. Shizentai
Right Chudan Zuki

20. Left Chudan Uchi-Uke

21.

22. Yoko Keage
Uraken Uchi

23. Turn

+ **24.** Kokutsu-Dachi
Left Chudan Shuto-Uke

+ **25.** Kokutsu-Dachi
Right Chudan Shuto-Uke

+ **26.** Kokutsu-Dachi
Left Chudan Shuto-Uke

+ **27.**

+ **32.** Turn

+ **33.** Kokutsu-Dachi
Manji-Gamae

+ **34.** Zenkutsu-Dachi Left Nagashi-Uke
Right Gedan Shuto-Uchi

+ **35.**

+ **40.** Turn

+ **41.** Kokutsu-Dachi
Manji-Gamae

+ **42.** Zenkutsu-Dachi
Left Nagashi-Uke
Right Gedan Shuto-Uchi

+ **43.** Renoji-Dachi
Gedan-Gamae

28. *Zenkutsu-Dachi Right Chudan Shihon Nukite. Kiai!*

29. *Turn*

30. *Gyaku-Hanmi Right Jodan Shuto-Uchi*

31. *Right Jodan Mae-Geri*

36. *Renoji-Dachi Gedan-Gamae*

37.

38. *Gyaku-Hanmi Right Jodan Shuto-Uchi*

39. *Right Jodan Mae-Geri*

44. *Turn*

45. *Left Yoko-Keage Uraken-Uchi*

46. *Zenkutsu-Dachi Mae-Empi*

47. *Turn Koshi-Gamae*

48. Right Yoko-Keage
Uraken-Uchi

49. Zenkutsu-Dachi
Mae-Empi

50. Turn

51. Kokutsu-Dachi
Left Shuto-Uke

56. Turn

57. Gyaki-Hanmi
Jodan Shuto-Uchi

58. Right Jodan Mae-Geri

59.

64. Turn

65. Kata-Ashi-Dachi
Right Ura-Zuki
Hiza Gamae

66. Morote Hiji Tate Fuse

67. Kokutsu-Dachi
Morote Gedan Shuto-Uke
Turn

52. *Kokutsu-Dachi Right Chudan Shuto-Uke*

53. *Turn*

54. *Kokutsu-Dachi Right Chudan Shuto-Uke*

55. *Kokutsu-Dachi Left Chudan Shuto-Uke*

60. *Kosa-Dachi Right Chudan Uraken-Uchi*

61. *Zenkutsu-Dachi Right Chudan Uchi-Uke*

62. *Zenkutsu-Dachi Left Chudan Gyaku-Zuki*

63. *Right Chudan-Zuki*

67a. *Side view of fig.67*

68. *Kokutsu-Dachi Right Chudan Shuto-Uke*

69. *Turn*

70. *Zenkutsu-Dachi Left Chudan Uchi-Uke*

┼ **71.** *Right Gyaku-Zuki*

┼ **72.** *Turn*

┼ **73.** *Zenkutsu-Dachi Right Chudan Uchi-Uke*

┼ **74.** *Left Gyaku-Zuki*

┼ **79.** *Kokutsu-Dachi Left Chudan Shuto-Uke*

┼ **80.** *Zenkutsu-Dachi Nihon Nukite*

⊕ **81.** *Turn*

⊕ **82.** *Turn*

┼ **87.** *Kiba-Dachi Koshi-Gamae*

┼ **88.** *Right Gedan-Barai*

┼ **88a.** *Side view of fig. 88*

┼ **89.**

75. Right Chudan-Zuki

76. Turn
Koshi-Gamae

77. Yoko-Keage
Uraken-Uchi

78. Turn

83. Kiba-Dachi
Left Jodan Uraken-Uchi

84.

85. Kiba-Dachi
Left Chudan Tetsui-Uchi

86. Kiba-Dachi
Empi-Uchi

89a. Side view of fig. 89

90. Kiba-Dachi
Ryo Ude Mawashi-Uke

90a. Side view of fig. 90

91. Kiba-Dachi
Right Otoshi-Zuki

91a. *Side view of fig. 91*

92.

92a. *Side view of fig. 92*

93. *Shizentai Jodan Shuto Juji-Uke*

96.

96a. *Front view of fig. 96*

97. *Nidan Tobi-Geri. Kiai!*

97a. *Front view of fig. 97*

102. *Yame*

93a. *Side view of fig. 93*

94. *Turn*

95. *Moto-Dachi*
Juji Gamae

95a. *Front view of fig. 95*

98. *Zenkutsu-Dachi*
Right Chudan Uraken-
Uchi

99. *Yame*

100. *Yame*

101. *Yame*

Kanku-Dai
APPLICATIONS

Figs 4-8 *Deflect opponent's first punch, simultaneously block second punch and strike to elbow joint*

Figs 4-8 *(alternative bunkai) Deflect opponent's first punch. He attempts to grab your legs to throw you. Counter palm-heel strike to ear and ox-hand strike to side of neck or face*

Figs 9-10 *Block punch and strike with knife-hand to neck or temple*

Figs 4-8 (second alternative bunkai) Deflect punch, grasp wrist and twist, strike to joint

Figs 9-10 (alternative bunkai) Move inside attack and strike with back of forearm to face

Figs 34-36 *Deflect punch and strike to groin. Simultaneously block second punch and sweep opponent's front leg*

Figs 56-60 *Deflect kick and counter with knife-hand to neck, grasp throat, kick to groin or stomach, move in and strike face with back-fist*

Figs 64-66 *Simultaneously block opponent's kick with raised leg and strike to jaw. Drop down and up-end opponent by seizing his legs*

Figs 67-88 *Block kick with knife-hand block, step in and counter knife-hand strike to neck or temple*

a   *b*   *c*

Figs 80-86 *Opponent attempts to apply wrist-lock. Turn under and strike with back-fist to face, hammer-fist to ribs, then grasp head and*

a   *b*   *c*

Figs 90-95 *Block kick and strike to ankle, block punch, grasp arm and turn to apply armlock, finish with back elbow strike to solar plexus*

g

a

Figs 99-102 *Opponent attacks from rear*

e

f

strike with elbow

e

f

c

d

with a kick. Block and scoop the leg high into the air

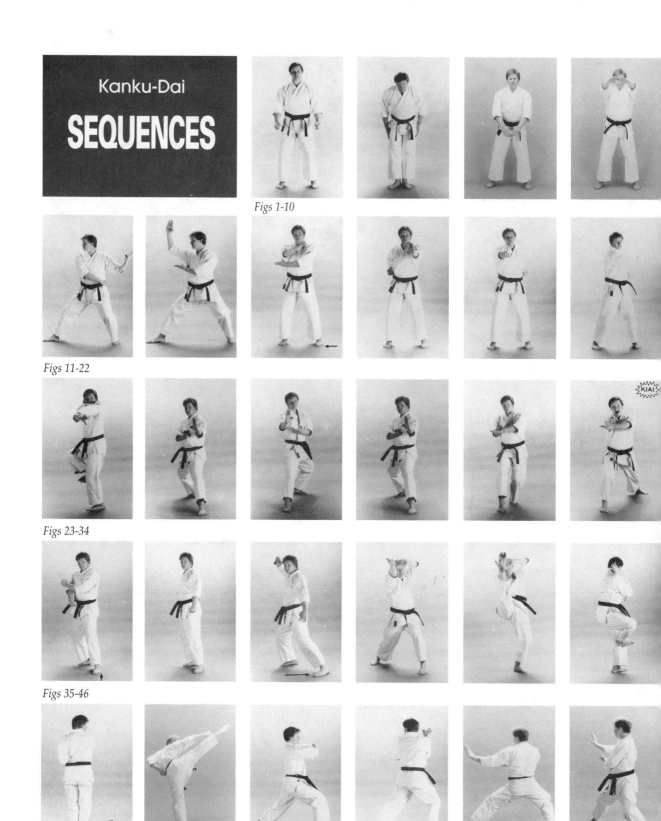

Kanku-Dai
SEQUENCES

Figs 1-10

Figs 11-22

Figs 23-34

Figs 35-46

Figs 47-58

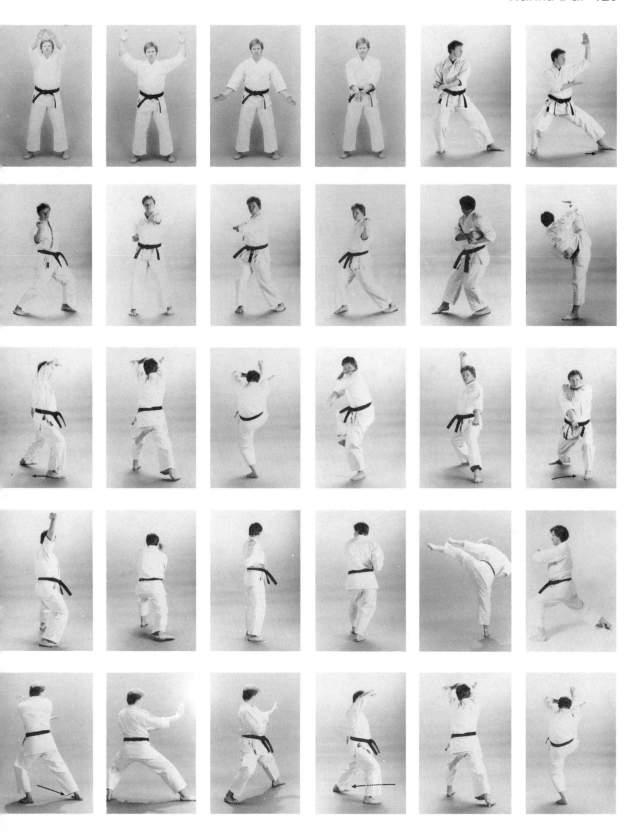

Figs 59-70

Figs 71-82

Figs 83-94

Figs 95-103

Empi

An early Kata, formerly known as *Hanshu*, the form we have today owes much to the revisions made by Yasutsune Itosu. The name was changed by Master Funakoshi following his introduction of Karate into the Japanese martial arts ethos. He chose the name *Empi* (also sometimes written as *Enpi* due to the idiosyncratic nature of Japanese pronunciation) as being descriptive of the erratic flight of a swallow, reflecting the up-and-down, forward and back, pattern of moves within the Kata.

This Kata is also unusual in that it contains feinting techniques, inviting an opponent to attack supposed weaknesses in defence.

1. *Shizentai*

2. *Yoi*

3. *Turn*

8. *Turn. Kiba-Dachi*
Left Kage-Zuki

9. *Step forwards*

10. *Zenkutsu-Dachi*
Gedan-Barai

11. *Zenkutsu-Dachi*
Jodan Age-Zuki

16. *Zenkutsu Dachi*
Left Gedan-Barai

17. *Zenkutsu-Dachi*
Right Jodan Age-Zuki

18. *Zenkutsu-Dachi*
Kami-Zukami

19. *Slide forwards*
Hiza-Geri

4. *Hiza-Dachi Right Gedan Barai Left Ken Mune Mae-Gamae*

5. *Step backwards*

6. *Shizentai Koshi-Gamae*

7. *Turn. Zenkutsu-Dachi Gedan-Barai*

12. *Zenkutsu-Dachi Kami-Zukami*

13. *Slide forwards Hiza-Geri*

14. *Kosa-Dachi Right Nagashi-Uke Left Otoshi-Zuki*

15. *Turn Ushiro Gedan-Barai*

20. *Kosa-Dachi Right Nagashi-Uke Left Otoshi-Zuki*

21. *Turn Ushiro Gedan-Barai*

22. *Zenkutsu-Dachi Gedan-Barai*

23. *Pull back*

24.

25. Kiba-Dachi
Jodan Haishu-Uke

KIAI

26. Kata-Ashi-Dachi
Empi-Uchi. Kiai!

27. Kiba-Dachi

32. Zenkutsu-Dachi
Jodan Age-Zuki

33. Step forwards

34. Kokutsu-Dachi
Right Shuto-Uke

35. Pull back front foot

40. Turn

41. Zenkutsu-Dachi
Gedan-Barai

42. Zenkutsu-Dachi
Right Jodan Age-Zuki

43. Zenkutsu-Dachi
Kami-Zukami

28. *Kiba-Dachi Left Chudan Tate Shuto-Uke*

29. *Kiba-Dachi Right Chudan-Zuki*

30. *Kiba-Dachi Left Chudan-Zuki*

31. *Turn. Zenkutsu-Dachi Gedan-Barai*

36. *Step forwards Kokutsu-Dachi Left Shuto-Uke*

37. *Kokutsu-Dachi Chudan Gyaku-Zuki*

38. *Step forwards*

39. *Kokutsu-Dachi Right Shuto-Uke*

44. *Hiza-Geri*

45. *Kosa-Dachi Right Nagashi-Uke Left Otoshi-Zuki*

46. *Turn Ushiro Gedan-Barai*

47. *Zenkutsu-Dachi Gedan-Barai*

48.

49. *Zenkutsu-Dachi* *Right Teisho-Uke*

50. *Step forwards*

51. *Step forwards*

56. *Kokutsu-Dachi* *Right Gedan-Barai*

56a. *Side view of fig. 56*

57. *Slide forwards* *Kiba-Dachi* *Morote Koko-Gamae*

57a. *Side View of fig. 57*

52. Zenkutsu-Dachi
Teisho Kosa-Uke

53. *Step forward Zenkutsu-
Dachi Teisho Kosa-Uke*

54. *Step forwards Zenkutsu-
Dachi Teisho Kosa-Uke*

55. *Slide forwards*

58. *Jump. Turn 360°
Kiai!*

59. Kokutsu-Dachi
Right Shuto-Uke

60. *Step backwards*
Kokutsu-Dachi
Left Shuto Uke

61. *Step backwards*
Yame

Empi

APPLICATIONS

a

b

Figs 2-8 *(alternative bunkai) Block kick and punch, counter with back fist strike. Step in*

f

g

d

strongly, throw him to the ground

a

Figs 6-8 *Step in and block opponent's kick,*

and block further punch, counter with hook punch to stomach

Figs 4-6 *Opponent attacks whilst you are in seated or kneeling position. Deflect kick strongly to unbalance him. Seize his head and twisting*

with same hand deflect his following punch. Counter with hook punch to stomach

Figs 17-21 Simultaneously block punch and strike to jaw. Continue with finger jab to eyes or grasp hair to pull opponent onto knee strike,

Figs 17-21 (alternative bunkai). Follow simultaneous block and punch, grab opponent's lapel and pull him onto kick to stomach, slide in and punch to mid section whilst blocking his counter punch, twist away and strike to head with hammer-fist

simultaneous knee strike (or use knee lift to guard groin from attack)

Figs 48-52 Opponent seizes your wrist, twist and press down attacker's wrist. Step in

follow with punch. Opponent grasps your punching arm, break grip by striking strongly with downward block

Figs 23-26 Lift leg to avoid opponent's sweep attack, block punch and grasp his head. Pull opponent onto elbow, attack head with

attacking simultaneously his wrist with left palm-heel and his jaw with right

Figs 50-52 Catch opponent's attacking arm and apply lock to elbow joint

Figs 56-57 Slide inside and block opponent's

Figs 56-57 (alternative bunkai). If opponent attacks with reverse punch, block and slide in, grasp him by groin and back of neck and throw

ront kick. Grasp him by throat and groin and throw with shoulder-wheel throw

Empi

SEQUENCES

Figs 1-10

Figs 11-24

Figs 25-36

Figs 37-48

Figs 49-61

KIAI

Sochin

There is some evidence that this Kata was devised by Ankichi Aragaki, and for some time it was known as *Hakko*. The development within *Shotokan* seems to owe much to the influence of Yoshitaka (Gigo) Funakoshi.

The most obvious feature of this Kata is the prominence given to the practice of *Fudo-dachi*, or *Sochin-dachi*, the 'rooted' or 'immovable' stance.

Sharing some similarities with *Hangetsu*, the feeling of the Kata is of being calmly and powerfully rooted to the Earth, unmovable in the face of the greatest danger *(Fudo-shin)*, and the strong stable stance provides a powerful base for the resistance of attacks from all quarters.

The execution of this Kata should not be rushed, but should demonstrate the shift from relaxed awareness to full tension. In some instances this should be a gradual process, and in others an instantaneous shift.

In parts there should be a sense of pressing home a succession of counterattacks which allow the opponent no time to respond.

Sochin
STEP BY STEP

+ **1.** Shizentai

+ **2.** Musubi-Dachi
Rei

+ **3.** Yoi

+ **8.** Sochin-Dachi Right
Chudan Tate Shuto-Uke

+ **9.** Sochin-Dachi
Left Chudan-Zuki

+ **10.** Sochin-Dachi
Right Gyaku-Zuki

+

+ **16.** Sochin-Dachi
Left Chudan-Zuki

+ **17.** Sochin-Dachi
Right Chudan Gyaku-Zuki

+ **18.** Turn

+ **19.** Kokutsu-Dachi
Manji-Gamae

4.

5.

6. Sochin-Dachi
Muso-Gamae

7. Step forward

12. Kokutsu-Dachi
Manji-Gamae

13. Step forward

14. Sochin-Dachi
Muso-Gamae

15. Sochin-Dachi Right
Chudan Tate Shuto-Uke

20. Sochin-Dachi
Muso-Gamae

21. Sochin-Dachi
Right Chudan Tate
Shuto-Uke

22. Sochin-Dachi
Left Chudan-Zuki

23. Sochin-Dachi
Right Chudan
Gyaku-Zuki

24. Turn
Koshi-Gamae

25. Yoko-Keage
Uraken-Uchi

26. Sochin-Dachi
Right Empi-Uchi

27. Turn
Koshi-Gamae

32. Kokutsu-Dachi
Left Chudan Shuto-Uke

33. Turn. Kokutsu-Dachi
Left Chudan Shuto-Uke

34. Kokutsu-Dachi
Right Chudan Shuto-Uke

35. Turn. Kokutsu-Dachi
Right Chudan Shuto-Uke

38a. Side view of fig. 38

39. Right Mae-Geri
Right Nagashi-Uke
Left Uraken-Uchi or Ura-
Zuki

39a. Side view of fig. 39

KIAI

40. Sochin-Dachi
Left Nagashi-Uke
Right Uraken-Uchi or Ur
Zuki. Kiai!

28. Yoko-Keage
Uraken-Uchi

29. Sochin-Dachi
Left Empi-Uchi

30. Turn

31. Kokutsu-Dachi
Right Chudan Shuto-Uke

36. Kokutsu-Dachi
Right Chudan Shuto-Uke

37. Slide forward
Left Osae-Uke Right Nukite

37a. Side view of fig. 37

38. Left Mae-Geri

40a. Side view of fig. 40

41. Turn
Right Jodan
Mikazuki-Geri

42. Sochin-Dachi
Muso-Gamae

43. Step

✝ **44.** *Sochin-Dachi Left Uchi-Uke*

✝ **45.** *Step*

✝ **46.** *Sochin-Dachi Right Chudan Oi-Zuki*

✝ **47.** *Turn*

✝ **52.** *Sochin-Dachi Gyaku-Hanmi Right Uchi-Uke*

✝ **53.** *Mae-Geri*

✝ **54.** *Sochin-Dachi Left Yumi-Zuki*

✝ **55.** *Sochin-Dachi Right Chudan Gyaku-Zu*

48. *Sochin-Dachi Right Uchi-Uke*

49. *Sochin-Dachi Left Chudan Oi-Zuki*

50. *Sochin-Dachi Left Uchi-Uke*

51.

56. *Sochin-Dachi Left Chudan Zuki. Kiai!*

57. *Yame*

Sochin

APPLICATIONS

a

b

Figs 5-10 Block opponent's kick, step in and simultaneously block punch and strike to groin,

f

g

a

b

c

Figs 36-40 Block punch, slide in and simultaneously block second punch and counter with straight fingers to throat. Follow with front

d

e

...sh away opponent, step in and punch twice to mid-section

e

foot kick then step in, block, strike with backfist or close punch to face and kick to stomach

Figs 41-42 *Deflect punch and attack the shoulder joint with crescent kick. Step in and block second punch. Strike to groin with hammer-fist*

Figs 50-56 *Block punch with wide block, block second punch, grasp arm and pull opponent on to front kick and punch to throat. Finish*

with two more punches to body

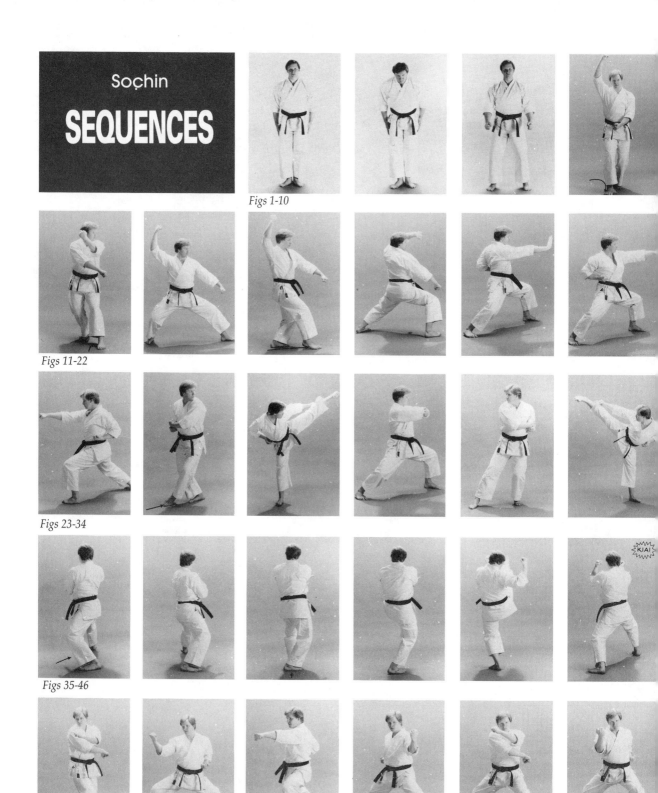

Soçhin

SEQUENCES

Figs 1-10

Figs 11-22

Figs 23-34

Figs 35-46

Fig 47-57

KIAI

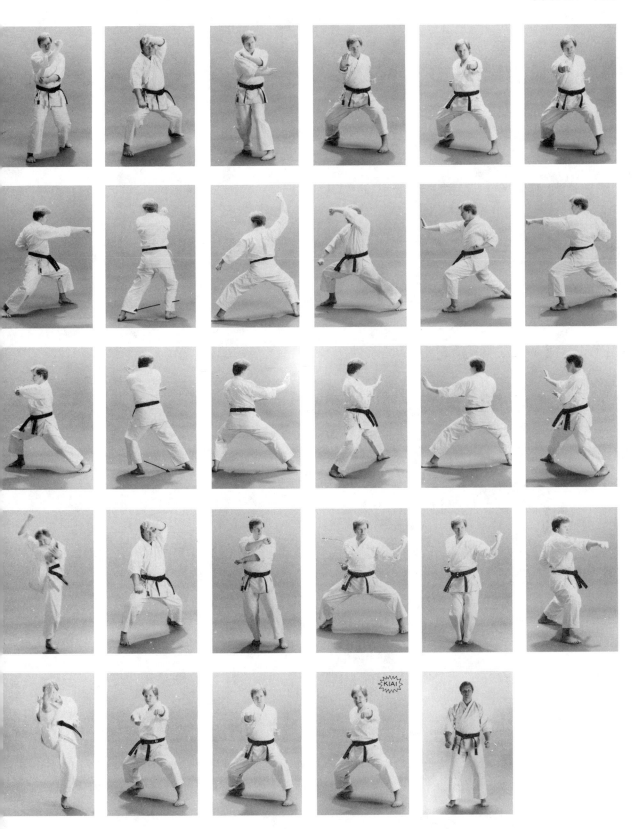

Jion

It is thought possible that this Kata was developed either in the Chinese Buddhist temple called *Jion* or by someone associated with the Temple, where it is known that the practice of martial arts was encouraged.

Of the 15 Kata which Funakoshi Gichin selected as the basis of his *Shotokan* Karate, and published in *Karate-do Kyohan*, only *Jion* and *Jutte* (10 hands) have kept their original names.

A version of this Kata is also practised in *Wado-ryu*.

In keeping with its Buddhist connotations, this Kata should be performed calmly, precisely and strongly, taking approximately one minute.

A useful Kata in the practice of defense against both armed and unarmed opponents, demanding precisely-aimed and focused blocks and counters.

Jion

STEP BY STEP

1. *Shizentai*

2. *Musubi-Dachi*

3. *Rei*

8. *Zenkutsu-Dachi Kakiwake-Uke*

9. *Mae-Geri*

10. *Zenkutsu-Dachi Right Chudan-Zuki*

11. *Zenkutsu-Dachi Left Gyaku-Zuki*

16. *Zenkutsu Dachi Left Chudan-Zuki*

17. *Zenkutsu-Dachi Right Gyaku-Zuki*

18. *Zenkutsu-Dachi Left Chudan-Zuki*

19. *Step forward*

4. *Yoi*

5.

6. *Step back Zenkutsu-Dachi Kosa-Uke*

7. *Step*

12. *Zenkutsu-Dachi Right Chudan-Zuki*

13. *Step*

14. *Zenkutsu-Dachi Kakiwake-Uke*

15. *Mae-Geri*

20. *Zenkutsu-Dachi Left Age-Uke*

21. *Zenkutsu-Dachi Right Chudan Gyaku-Zuki*

22. *Step forward*

23. *Zenkutsu-Dachi Right Age-Uke*

+ **24.** *Zenkutsu-Dachi*
Left Chudan Gyaku-Zuki

+ **25.** *Step forward*

+ **26.** *Zenkutsu-Dachi*
Left Age-Uke

+ **27.** *Zenkutsu-Dachi*
Oi-Zuki. Kiai!

KIAI

+ **31.** *Turn*

+ **32.** *Kokutsu-Dachi*
Manji-Uke

+ **33.** *Kiba-Dachi*
Left Chudan Kage-Zuki

+ **33a.** *Front view of fig.*

+ **38.** *Step forwards*

+ **39.** *Kiba-Dachi*
Left Chudan Teisho-Uchi

+ **39a.** *Front view of fig. 39*

+ **40.** *Step forwards*

28. *Turn*

29. *Kokutsu-Dachi*
Manji-Uke

30. *Kiba-Dachi*
Right Chudan Kage-Zuki

30a. *Front view of fig. 30*

34. *Step*

35. *Zenkutsu-Dachi*
Gedan-Barai

36. *Step forwards*

37. *Kiba-Dachi*
Right Chudan Teisho-Uchi

41. *Kiba-Dachi*
Right Chudan Teisho-Uchi

42. *Turn*

43. *Kokutsu-Dachi*
Manji-Uke

44.

45. Heisoku-Dachi
Jodan Morote-Uke

46. Turn

47. Kokutsu-Dachi
Manji-Uke

48.

53. Kosa-Dachi
Gedan Juji-Uke

54. Slide backwards Zenkutsu-
Dachi Ryowan Gedan Kakiwake

55. Step forwards

56. Zenkutsu-Dachi
Sowan Uchi-Uke

61. Turn

62. Zenkutsu-Dachi
Left Uchi-Uke

63. Step forwards
Zenkutsu-Dachi
Right Chudan Oi-Zuki

64. Turn

49. *Heisoku-Dachi Jodan Morote-Uke*

50. *Turn*

51. *Heisoku-Dachi Ryowan-Gamae*

52. *Slide forward*

57. *Step forwards Zenkutsu-Dachi Jodan Juji-Uke*

58. *Zenkutsu-Dachi Left Jodan Age-Uke Right Ura-Zuki*

59. *Zenkutsu-Dachi Right Jodan Nagashi-Uke Left Chudan Zuki-Uke*

60. *Zenkutsu-Dachi Right Jodan Ura-Zuki*

65. *Zenkutsu-Dachi Right Uchi-Uke*

66. *Step forwards Zenkutsu-Dachi Left Oi-Zuki*

67. *Turn*

68. *Zenkutsu-Dachi Left Gedan-Barai*

+ **69.** Step forwards

+ **70.** Kiba-Dachi Right
Otoshi-Uke Doji-Fumikomi

+ **71.** Step forwards

+ **72.** Kiba-Dachi Left
Otoshi-Uke Doji-Fumikon

+ **76.** Slide

+ **77.** Kiba-Dachi
Left Yumi-Zuki

+ **78.** Turn Kiba-Dachi
Jodan Tsukami-Uke

+ **79.** Slide

72a. *Front view of fig. 72*

73. *Step forward*

74. *Kiba-Dachi Right Otoshi-Uke Doji-Fumikomi*

75. *Turn Jodan Tsukami-Uke*

KIAI

80. *Kiba-Dachi Right Yumi-Zuki. Kiai!*

81.

82. *Yame.*

Jion

APPLICATIONS

a

b

Figs 4-6 *Block opponent's kick with downward block and strike to jaw with close punch*

b

c

d

lapels. Break grip by forcing his arms apart and push opponent back. Follow with front kick and rapid series of punches

a

b

c

Figs 32-33 *Block opponent's kick, focusing both arms, block punch, slide in and counter with hook punch*

Figs 7-12 *Opponent attempts to grab your*

f

g

Figs 35-41 Block opponent's punch, step in and strike to solar plexus with palm-heel. Step back and block second punch, hook away

Figs 43-45 Block attacker's kick, step inside punch and simultaneously block and counter with close punch

Figs 52-60 Block front kick and slide back and disengage from his attempt to grab your arms. Attacker then attempts to seize your lapels. Break

e f

attacking arm, step and strike once more with palm-heel

e f

his grip with double inside block. Your opponent continues with a series of punches which you simultaneously block and counter, finishing

with close-punch to the jaw

Figs 67-69 Block punch and grasp arm. Step in and strike to neck or shoulder joint. Grasp neck and thrust head to the ground whilst

Figs 74-76 Deflect punch, slide in and strike with hammer fist

sweeping away supporting leg

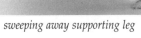

e

b

c

Figs 77-79 *Deflect punch and grasp wrist. Slide in and counter punch to ribs*

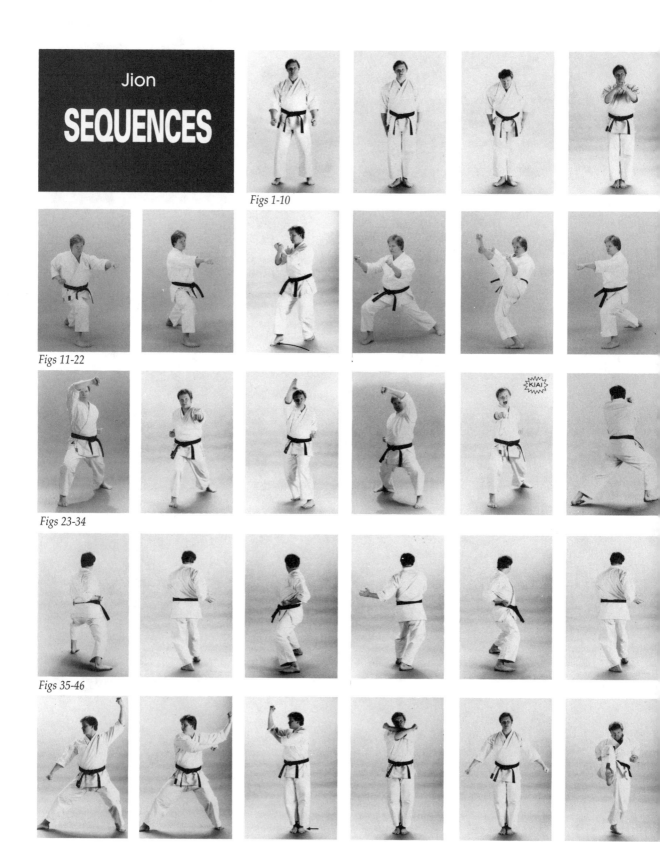

Jion
SEQUENCES

Figs 1-10

Figs 11-22

Figs 23-34

Figs 35-46

Figs 47-58

Figs 59-70

Figs 71-82

Hangetsu

Originally called *Seishan*, this Kata is now known as *Hangetsu* (half-moon) because of the crescent-shaped movements of the feet and the semi-circular hand techniques. This Kata originated in the *Naha-te* system, and is characterised with fast, sharp counter-attacks.

The early genesis of the Kata is demonstrated by its emphasis on pragmatic applications of close range self-defence techniques, with the sliding foot movements being used to close the gap with an opponent and destroy his balance and stability, and thus the strength of his attack.

The Kata should take approximately one minute to perform.

Hangetsu
STEP BY STEP

$\perp$ **1.** *Shizentai*

$\perp$ **2.** *Musubi-Dachi*

$\perp$ **3.** *Rei*

$\perp$ **8.** *Step forwards*

$\perp$ **9.** *Hangetsu-Dachi Right Chudan Uchi-Uke*

$\perp$ **10.** *Hangetsu-Dachi Left Chudan Gyaku-Zuki*

$\perp$ **11.** *Step forward*

$\perp$ **16.** *Pull back*

$\perp$ **17.**

$\perp$ **18.** *Hangetsu-Dachi Chudan Ippon-Ken*

$\perp$ **19.**

4. *Yoi*

5. *Step forwards*

6. *Hangetsu-Dachi Left Chudan Uchi-Uke*

7. *Hangetsu-Dachi Right Chudan Gyaku-Zuki*

12. *Hangetsu-Dachi Left Chudan Uchi-Uke*

13. *Hangetsu-Dachi Right Chudan Gyaku-Zuki*

14. *Left fist to right wrist Ippon Ken*

15. *Left fist to right wrist Ippon Ken*

20. *Hangetsu-Dachi Kaishu Yama-Gamae*

21.

22. *Hangetsu-Dachi Kaishu Ryowan-Gamae*

23. *Turn*

KIAI

24. *Hangetsu-Dachi Kaishu-Kosa-Uke. Kiai!*

25. *Hangetsu-Dachi Right Kake-Dori*

26. *Step forwards Hangetsu-Dachi Kaishu-Kosa-Uke*

27. *Hangetsu-Dachi Left Kake-Dori*

30. *Turn*

31. *Slide. Hangetsu-Dachi Right Uchi-Uke Chudan*

32. *Left Gyaku-Zuki*

33. *Right Chudan-Zuki*

38. *Turn*

39. *Slide. Hangetsu-Dachi Right Uchi-Uke Chudan*

40. *Left Gyaku-Zuki*

41. *Right Chudan Zuki*

28. Hangetsu-Dachi
Kaishu-Kosa-Uke

28a. Front view of fig. 28

29. Hangetsu-Dachi
Right Kake-Dori

29a. Front view of fig. 29

34. Turn

35. Slide. Hangetsu-Dachi
Left Uchi-Uke Chudan

36. Right Gyaku-Zuki

37. Left Chudan Zuki

42. Turn

43. Turn

44. Turn

45. Kokutsu-Dachi
Chudan Uraken Gamae

46. *Hanmi Sashi-Ashi*

47. *Doji Hazushite Left Mae-Geri*

48. *Hangetsu-Dachi Left Gedan-Barai*

49. *Hangetsu-Dachi Right Chudan Gyaku-Zuki*

54. *Hanmi Sashi-Ashi*

55. *Doji Hazushite Right Mae-Geri*

56. *Hangetsu-Dachi Right Gedan-Barai*

57. *Left Chudan Gyaku-Zuki*

62. *Right Mikazuki-Geri. Kiai!*

63. *Zenkutsu-Dachi Right Gedan Gyaku-Zuki*

64. *Pull back*

65. *Neko Ashi-Dachi Teisho Awase Gedan-Uke*

50. Left
Age-Uke

51. Turn

52. Turn

53. Kokutsu-Dachi
Chudan Uraken Gamae

58. Right
Age-Uke

59. Turn

60. Turn

61. Kokutsu-Dachi
Chudan Uraken Gamae

66. Yame

Hangetsu

APPLICATIONS

a   *b*

Figs 14-22 Opponent grabs from the rear. Thrust fists sharply forwards and then back to

f   *g*   *a*

Figs 24-25 Block punching attack and or any appropriate technique

b   *c*   *d*

Snap leg up out of the way and step in to jam his punch with your forearm. Opponent seizes wrist. Pull back sharply and kick to stomach,

strike his hands with thumb knuckle joints. Thrust fists forward again and up to break grip, counter with knife-hand strike to the groin

grasp arm. Pull to break balance, step in and counter with straight fingers to the throat   **Fig 42-50** *Opponent attacks with leg sweep.*

step in blocking his counter punch and strike with reverse punch. He attacks again with a punch. Block with upward block and finish with any

h *appropriate counter*   **i**   **a** **Figs 52-58** *Lift leg to avoid foot sweep.*

e   **f**   **g**

block. Block his next punch with downward block and counter with roundhouse elbow strike

d   **e**   **f**

Drop down and scoop up his leg to throw him and punch to his exposed groin or mid-section. Maintain your guard in case he continues to

Step in to jam opponent's punch. As he punches again, simultaneously attack with front kick whilst blocking the punch with forearm

igs 59-65 Lift leg to avoid foot sweep. Block punch attack. Grasp attacker's arm and kick to side of head with crescent kick to unbalance him.

attack from the floor

Hangetsu

SEQUENCES

Figs 1-11

Figs 12-24

Figs 25-38

Figs 39-52

Figs 53-66

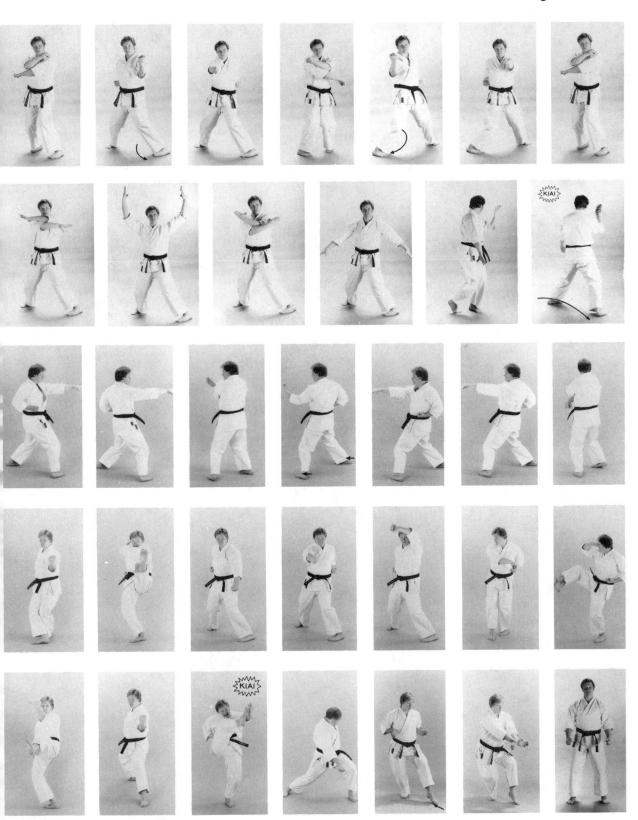

二十四步

Nijushiho

Like *Sochin*, this Kata appears to have been created by Ankichi Aragaki, and was formerly known as *Niseishi*.

Nakayama *sensei* tells of being taken by Master Funakoshi in 1934 to learn this Kata and *Gojushiho* from Kenwa Mabuni, the founder of *Shito-ryu* Karate, and that their forms were gradually altered to conform with the techniques being practised in *Shotokan*.

Meaning literally 'Twenty-four steps', in its varied application of tension and relaxation, and immediate transition from slow application of *Kime* to rapid execution of consecutive techniques, it shares some of the characteristics of *Sochin*.

The Kata affords practice in various grasping and countering techniques, and employs much use of elbow and open-hand blocks and counters, and demonstrates the use of distraction to gain advantage.

Some early forms make no use of the current grasp and side-kick combination, but use the upraised leg as a deflection or block, bringing the attacker into close range for the counter-punch. The modern version relies on the greater degree of athleticism now required of the *Karate-ka*. Both forms can be usefully practical, however you should avoid the temptation to use the modern version as an opportunity to demonstrate flexibility, and take care to strike directly at a realistic target.

Nijushiho

STEP BY STEP

1. *Shizentai*

2. *Heisoku-Dachi Rei*

3. *Yoi*

8. *Slide forwards*

9. *Left Shizentai Empi-Uchi*

10. *Turn*

11.

14a. *Front view of fig. 14*

15. *Step forwards*

15a. *Front view of fig. 15*

16. *Zenkutsu-Dachi Kakiwake-Uke*

4.

5. *Slide backwards*

6. *Kokutsu-Dachi*
Ryusui No Kamae

7. *Kokutsu-Dachi*
Ryusui-Zuki Slide forwards

12. *Sanchin-Dachi*
Ryo Goshi-Gamae

13. *Sanchin-Dachi*
Awase-Zuki

13a. *Front view of fig. 13*

14. *Ryowan Jodan*
Hasami-Uke Hiza-Gamae

16a. *Front view of fig. 16.*

17. *Turn*

18. *Zenkutsu-Dachi*
Left Jodan Age-Uke

19. *Zenkutsu-Dachi*
Right Tate-Empi

<table>
<tr><td>— 20. Turn</td><td>— 21. Kiba-Dachi Right Chudan Tate Shuto-Uke</td><td>— 22. Migi Ken Migi Koshi Yoko-Geri Kekomi</td><td>— 23. Kiba-Dachi Left Chudan-Zuki</td></tr>
<tr><td>28. Pull back foot</td><td>29. Right Chudan Kake-Uke</td><td>30. Step forwards</td><td>31. Zenkutsu-Dachi Teisho Awase-Zuki</td></tr>
<tr><td>36.</td><td>37. Fudo-Dachi Gedan Awase-Zuki</td><td>38. Kokutsu-Dachi</td><td>39. Left Haishu-Uke</td></tr>
</table>

24. *Turn*

25. *Kiba-Dachi Left Chudan Tate Shuto-Uke*

26. *Hidari Ken Hidari Goshi Koko-Geri Kekomi*

27. *Kiba-Dachi Right Chudan-Zuki*

32. *Turn. Zenkutsu-Dachi Right Jodan Haito-Uchi Left Gedan Teisho or Haito-Uke*

KIAI

33. *Heisoku-Dachi Left Haishu Age-Uchi. Kiai!*

34. *Step backwards*

35. *Zenkutsu-Dachi Koko Hiza Kuzushi*

40. *Step forwards Kiba-Dachi Right Jodan Tate-Empi*

41. *Slide Kiba-Dachi Right Jodan Soto-Uke Left Chudan-Zuki*

42. *Slide Kiba-Dachi Right Gedan-Barai*

43. *Turn*

44. *Kokutsu-Dachi Left Haishu-Uke*

45. *Step backwards Kiba-Dachi Right Mae-Empi*

46. *Kiba-Dachi Right Gedan-Barai Left Soete*

47. *Step forwards*

52. *Turn*

53. *Ofuri Kosa-Barai*

54. *Sanchin-Dachi Ryo Goshi-Gamae*

55. *Sanchin-Dachi Awase-Zuki. Kiai!*

60.

↙ **48.** *Kokutsu-Dachi Left Haishu-Uke*

↙ **49.** *Step forwards Kiba-Dachi Right Jodan Tate-Empi*

↙ **50.** *Slide Kiba-Dachi Right Jodan Soto-Uke Left Chudan-Zuki*

↙ **51.** *Slide Kiba-Dachi Right Gedan-Barai*

╀ **56.**

╀ **57.** *Step forwards*

╀ **58.** *Sanchin-Dachi Mawashi Kake-Uke*

╀ **59.** *Sanchin-Dachi Awase Teisho-Zuki*

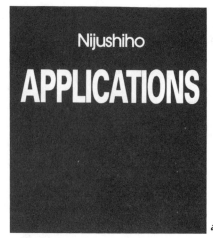

Nijushiho

APPLICATIONS

Figs 5-10 As opponent attacks, slide back and block punch, countering with reverse punch.

a

b

c

Figs 5-7 (alternative bunkai) As opponent attacks, slide back, catch arm twist and apply elbow lock.

a

b

c

Figs 5-10 (alternative bunkai) As opponent attacks, slide back and block punch. Grasp opponent's wrist and attack with upward forearm to

Gripping his arm, attack over the top with elbow strike to head

apply arm lock

Figs 15-17 Simultaneously block and strike to opponent's arm, applying an arm lock. Continue with front kick to stomach or groin and push

Figs 18-20 Block opponent's punch, step in and strike to head and jaw with elbow strikes

Figs 22-24 Block and seize opponent's arm, counter with side thrust kick to stomach or head, step in and punch to mid section

opponent away

Figs 18-20 *(alternative bunkai) Block opponent's punch, step in and strike to the jaw with upward elbow strike*

(alternative c)

Figs 29-32 (alternative bunkai) Block and press down opponent's punch, step in and counter simultaneously with palm-heel strike to head and

Figs 29-31 Deflect punch with palm-heel block, step in and counter with palm-heel strike to groin and chin

Figs 33-37 Startle opponent with large hand movement, duck and seize his leading leg to throw him to the ground; finish with any suitable

groin

b

c

Figs 32-33 *Simultaneously deflect kick and counter with ridge-hand strike, grab hair and strike with straight fingers to throat*

counter

e

f

Figs 39-42 *Deflect punch with back-hand block. Step in and counter with elbow strike to jaw and punch to stomach, slide away and strike to*

Figs 44-47 *Block opponent's punch with back-hand block, step in and strike to mid section with side elbow. Finish with back fist strike to the groin*

second attack and deflect with hooking block, counter with double palm-heel strike to groin and head

groin with bottom fist

a   b

Figs 52-59 *Block fist, punch and counter with double punch to head and solar plexus. Block*

g

Figs 55-58 *Following double punch, deflect and encircle opponent's counter, grasp neck or head and pull in and either apply arm lock or*

Figs 56-69 *Defending against lapel grab, in a circular motion entangle opponent's arms and continue to push away or throw*

strike to face with knee

e

e

Nijushiho
SEQUENCES

Figs 1-10

Figs 11-23

Figs 24-35

Figs 36-47

Figs 48-60

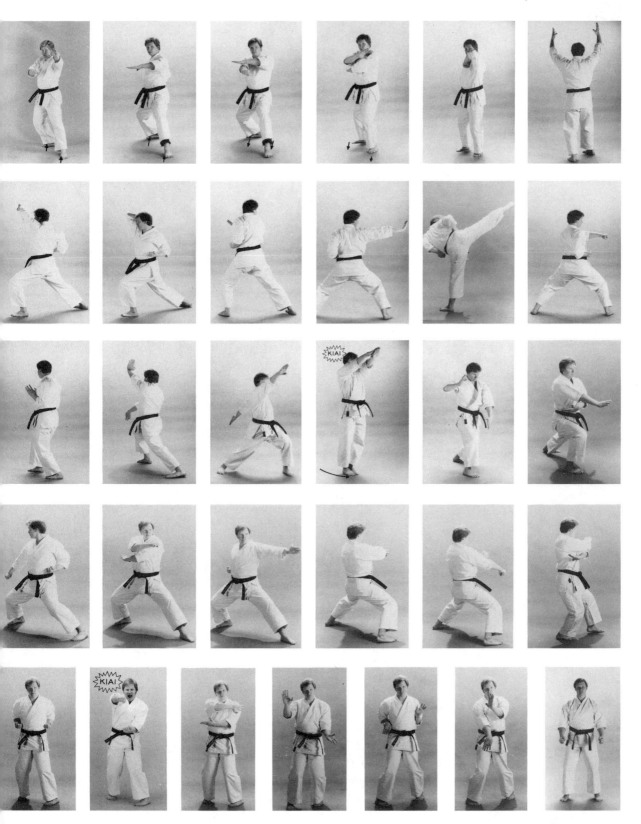

DATE DUE